7074

Everything You Need To Know About

LIVING WITH A
SINGLE
PARENT

Single-parent families need cooperation and compromise to run smoothly.

• THE NEED TO KNOW LIBRARY •

Everything You Need To Know About

LIVING WITH A SINGLE PARENT

Richard E. Mancini

THE ROSEN PUBLISHING GROUP, INC.
NEW YORK

Published in 1992, 1995 by The Rosen Publishing Group, Inc.
29 East 21st Street, New York,, New York 10010

Revised Edition 1995
Copyright © 1992, 1995 by The Rosen Publishing Group, Inc.

Printed in Canada

Library of Congress Cataloging-in-Publication Data

Mancini, Richard E.
    Everything you need to know about living with a single parent
    (The Need to know library)
    Includes bibliographical references and index.
    Summary: Discusses why some families have only one parent and
examines some of the problems that occur in single-parent families.
    ISBN 0-8239-2118-2
    1. Children of single parents—United States—Juvenile literature. [1.
Single-parent families. 2. Family problems. 3. Family life.]
I. Title. II .Series.
HQ777.4.M36   1991
306.85'6—dc20   91-28750
                                                          CIP
                                                           AC

Contents

Introduction

What does the word *family* mean to you? Most people picture a man, a woman, and their children. But the two-parent family is not the only kind of family. In many families, a single parent takes care of the children.

There are different kinds of single-parent families. After a divorce, one parent often cares for the children. The death of one parent leaves the other to carry on alone. Some single people adopt children and create a single-parent family. In some families, the mother has been the only parent the children have ever known. The father has never lived with the family.

There are more two-parent families than single-parent families in the United States. But the number of single-parent families is growing every year. Single-parent families present special problems for both the children and the parents. But there are good things, too. Each single-parent family has qualities that make it special.

This book is about the special things that happen in single-parent families. It explains the different problems that create single-parent families. It tells how to handle the problems that members of single-parent families have. This book also talks about something very important: Understanding that having only one parent does not make a family less loving, for either the parent or the child.

Many single women who become pregnant choose to raise a family on their own.

Chapter 1

You're Still a Family

The single-parent family is still very much a family, even though only one parent is present. Single parents and their children can experience all the love and joy of family life, as well as all the problems. Even though you may not have two parents, that does not mean that your family is any less loving or happy.

Single-parent homes are created in several ways. The most common way creates about two thirds of all single-parent families. That is when parents divorce. Sometimes one parent dies, leaving the other parent to cope on his or her own. And sometimes a parent chooses to raise a child on his or her own.

Starting Single

Some people have always lived in a single-parent home. Their parents are single by choice, not by chance. Sometimes a pregnant woman, often a teenager, decides to have her baby but does not get married. Sometimes the mother does not feel ready to get married, or does not want to marry the father of the child. Sometimes the parents break up before the child is born. And sometimes the mother is left to support the child alone.

Another way a child might be born into a single-parent home is through adoption. More and more single adults are deciding that they would like to adopt children, but that they do not want to get married.

Most people don't remember things that happen to them before they were two or three years old. So you might have lived with two parents before then, but not remember it. The parent you live with now may be the only one you remember.

Betsy, now 18, tells her thoughts about growing up in a single-parent home.

I liked living in a single-parent family. I always felt so much closer to my mom. She never had any distractions, and gave my sister and me all her attention. She would always spend time with us, and did special little things for us all the time. I guess she was trying extra hard to be a good parent, maybe to make up for our not having a dad around. But I never really felt like I wanted one. It's hard to miss what you never had.

Divorce

Sometimes parents feel that they simply cannot live together any more. They decide to get a divorce. Suddenly one of your parents isn't living with you any more. You're thrown into a single-parent family. You might be more comfortable if your home situation was unhappy before. Or you might be very angry, blaming yourself, blaming your parents.

It can be very difficult to adjust to living in a single-parent home created by divorce. It will be even more so if you do not accept that the divorce is final. Both your parents are having a hard time as it is; don't make it harder on them. It makes their task even more difficult to hear you yell about how unfair life is.

That doesn't mean that you shouldn't tell your parents how you feel. If you're unhappy, tell them. If you miss your parent, say so. If they are having problems coping with the divorce and are creating new problems for you, tell them that too. Reasonable communication can make a single-parent family a happy home. Without it, it's very hard to survive.

Death

When one parent dies, it is a great shock to the family. There is often no time to deal with the new

One of the most painful parts of living in a single-parent family is
missing the absent parent.

living situation, because everyone is trying to cope with their grief, loss, and fear.

If you lost a parent, it's important for everyone in your family to support one another. Your family can help each other adjust to life in a single-parent home. It is always hard to lose a parent, but if you all help each other out, you will be able to cope better than you each could alone.

You're Not the Only One

You might feel that living with a single parent makes you different from other kids. True, most kids do live in two-parent homes. But many do not. One out of two people under 18 either lives or has lived in a single-parent home at one time or another, and that number is growing. Millions of children live in single-parent families throughout the United States and Canada.

You aren't so different. Single-parent families are a part of life. You are not alone.

Many teens in single-parent families get part-time jobs or do chores to earn extra money for themselves or their families.

Chapter 2

Always Single

If you've always lived in a single-parent home, or if you've lived in one ever since you can remember, you may not be able to imagine what it would be like to have two parents. The idea may even seem strange to you.

You probably have a very special relationship with your parent. Throughout your life, your parent has always been there for you. You have always depended on him or her. Your one parent takes care of all your needs, and this has made the two of you feel very close. But supporting a family takes a lot of work and is hard to do alone. Your parent may not have a lot of time to spend with you. And you may have a lot more responsibilities than your friends.

You have the advantage over other single-parent families that you never had the trauma of losing a parent. You have grown up in your single-parent home, and don't need to learn how to survive in it. It's the only way of life you know.

"Real" Parents?

You may be very curious about your other parent. No one has only one parent; somewhere out there is another parent of yours whom you might have never met. The parent you live with might speak badly of your other parent, or might never speak of him or her at all. Whatever the case, it's only natural for you to wonder about your other parent.

If you were adopted, you might wonder about your birth parents. You might imagine them to be movie stars, or rich, or royalty. It's fun to make things up about your birth parents. But remember, your daydreams are probably much better than the real thing.

You might feel very strange around your parent when you think about being adopted. You might feel that you don't belong with him or her. You might want to find out who your "real" parents are.

Sometimes kids who were adopted don't realize that it takes more than giving birth to be a parent. That's why people who put their babies up for adoption are called birth parents, or *biological*

Taking time to understand each other's feelings is the most important thing parents and children can do together.

Single parents are often very busy, but it is important for them to take time to give their children love and affection.

parents. It isn't that hard to have a baby. The hard part is raising one. The parent you live with, the one who brought you up, took care of you, loves you very much—that's your "real" parent. You have more ties to him or her than just your genes.

That doesn't mean that your birth parents were bad people. They made the choice that they thought was best for you. For whatever reason, they thought you would be happier if you didn't live with them. Perhaps they had very little money. Perhaps they were very young, and not responsible enough to take care of you. They didn't give you up because they didn't love you, but because they did.

You shouldn't feel weird or unloved because you were adopted. You should feel special. After all, your parent chose you. He or she wanted a baby to love and decided to take you home. That should make you feel pretty good about yourself.

You might want to go looking for your birth parents. That is quite an undertaking, and you won't be able to find them unless they want to be found. Before you start on a project that will take a lot of time, a lot of effort, and a lot of trouble, and doesn't even guarantee that you'll succeed, think about your idea. Your parent loves you. Do you really need to find out who your birth parents are? You might not like what you find. And even if you don't find anything, your parent might be very hurt that you felt you needed to look. Talk it over with your real parent before you do anything.

Many children grow to like the feeling of being a "team" with their single parent.

Just You and Me

Together, you and your parent face the world. You may like the feeling of taking on the world with your single parent.

But your parent has needs that you can't fill. Your parent needs adult companionship too. He or she may want to have a relationship with another adult. This may make you uncomfortable. You may be afraid of losing the bond you have with your parent. You may not even like the people your parent dates.

Whether you like them or not, your parent has to decide whom he or she wants as a companion. You can't tell your parent who would be a good partner any more than he or she can tell you. And having a good relationship with another adult will make your parent a happier person. There is no limit on love. Don't worry that you will lose your parent. He or she will always be there for you.

You might have the opposite problem. You may feel that your parent depends on you too much. If your parent is trying to use you as a substitute for an adult confidant, you might feel uncomfortable. You might feel that your life is not your own.

Whatever your situation, it is important to communicate with your parent. Let him or her know how you're feeling. The more you understand each other, the better your relationship will be, and the happier your single-parent home will be.

Divorce is one of the most common creators of single-parent families, and a major source of painful emotions.

Chapter 3

Divorce Changes Everything and Everybody

Many single-parent families are created when a married couple divorces. A divorce legally ends a marriage. Husband and wife find separate places to live. Usually the children of a divorced couple live with one of the parents. That parent has *custody* of the children. That means the parent is responsible for caring for the children. When children begin living with the parent who has custody, they become part of a single-parent family.

Angry and Hurt

Divorce is usually a painful experience for everyone. This includes both of the parents and the children. If your parents have been divorced, you know how hurt and confused you can become. And suddenly living with only one parent can cause you all kinds of unhappy feelings. You will naturally miss your absent parent. But you may also feel some guilt about the divorce. You may think that you could have stopped it. You couldn't have. You may think that you caused it somehow. You didn't.

You might also be very angry with both your parents. You may blame them for splitting up your family. These feelings are natural. And they will take time to get over. During a divorce you need to talk to both your parents about your feelings and fears. By telling them how you really feel, you can help yourself. And you can help your family understand how you feel.

Whose Fault Is It?

People involved in a painful situation, like a divorce, look for someone to blame. If your parents have just divorced, they may be blaming each other. How should you feel when this happens?

A divorce can happen for many reasons. You might not understand all of the reasons. But you can try to accept what has happened to your family. A divorce is not only one person's fault. So you should try not to blame anyone. You may want to blame one of your parents for the divorce. But remember, a marriage takes two people. And so does a divorce. If you still feel very angry long after the divorce, you may need help to handle your feelings. You can talk with a counselor at school or at your place of worship.

Kate has lived with her mom in a single-parent family off-and-on for several years. Kate's father was violent and abusive. Her mom was divorced from her dad and got married again. Kate's stepfather wasn't violent, but he was very mean. Kate's mother divorced him too. Here, Kate talks about the blame for both divorces.

I blame my real father for the first divorce, and I blame myself for the second. My first dad was sick. He ruined our family. And he destroyed my mom's self-esteem. I blame myself for the second divorce. But not in a "bad" way. I should have told my mother not to live with him. If she had listened, we never would have had that trouble.

Finding blame for a divorce is a waste of time. It only helps you to think about bad feelings. It doesn't help you get on with your life. A couple gets a divorce because of *its* own problems—*not* because of something the children have said or done. Many children think that they have somehow caused their parents' divorce. This guilt makes children angry and depressed. They may turn to drugs to escape. Some may even attempt suicide. These people feel guilty about something they did not do.

Parents and children often grow very close in single-parent families. Sometimes they feel more like "friends" than family.

If you ever feel that something you did caused your parents to divorce, tell your parents your thoughts right away. They may not be aware of your feelings. They can reassure you that their divorce was not your fault. A divorce is between a husband and wife—not between parents and their children.

Everything's Changed

Families who go through a divorce often find their world turned "upside down." A divorce changes more than your living situation. It can also change how much money the family has to live on and where you go to school. All of these are drastic changes. And they often happen in a very short time. If your family is going through a divorce and starting a single-parent home, there will be a lot to get used to. You must try to accept changes in your life and learn how to deal with them.

• *Life without Dad (or Mom)* The biggest change after a divorce is the absence of one of your parents. You may miss your parent a lot. You will not see him or her every day as you used to.

• *Moving Away* Sometimes, a new single-parent family moves to a new home. This new place could be in the same town, or across the country. If your new home is in another town or state, it means more changes. You will have to get used to a new school and make new friends. You will miss your old friends.

• *A Broken Home* After a divorce, it may bother you to see other kids with "complete" families (both parents). You may keep asking yourself, "Why us? Why me?" Remember that millions of couples get divorced or separated. And there are millions of children just like you.

• *Living on Less* Both of your parents may have a lot less money after a divorce. They need to support two separate places to live. At least one of them will probably have to furnish a new home.

• *Two Sets of "Parents"* Some divorced couples are awarded joint custody of their children. The kids live with one parent part of the time and with the other parent at other times. This creates *two* single-parent families, instead of just one.

Talk about It

Your parents' divorce and all the changes it brings will upset you. Tell your parents how you feel. It may be hard to talk to both of them at the same time. But it's important that they both know how their divorce makes you feel. If you talk about your feelings, you will be able to adjust more easily to all the changes going on around you. Expressing yourself will help you feel more comfortable in your new single-parent situation.

The death of a parent can create a single-parent family very suddenly, before members can adjust to the idea.

Chapter 4

When a Parent Dies

The death of a parent is a great tragedy. It brings major changes to the life of a family. And it creates a single-parent family suddenly, without notice. This is a great shock to the surviving family. This loss is the most painful one a child can experience. Parents give their children love and security. Parents fulfill physical and material needs. They are the most important people in a child's life. Adjusting to life without a parent is very hard. The adjustment may take a long time. During this difficult time, the surviving parent and children need each other's support.

How Could It Happen to Us?

When a parent dies, a family feels shock, grief, and disbelief. These feelings occur whether the death was caused by an accident or by illness. It is

Mourning a dead parent is an important part of adjusting to a new single-parent family.

hard to believe that such a terrible thing could happen to you. At first you may not want to believe that one of your parents has died. People often deal with great shocks this way. It is natural to feel that it is all a bad dream.

When a parent dies your family's life is changed forever. You will miss the parent, you will remember all the things about him or her you may have taken for granted. Your family routine will be disrupted. You will no longer be able to share with your parent all the things you enjoyed. But your family's life will continue. Your suddenly single parent will need your love and help to keep the family going.

Dealing with the Feelings

The time following a parent's death will be tough. You and your family will share feelings of sadness, anger, fear, loss, and even guilt. These are all natural feelings for both adults and children. You may feel sad for quite a long time, knowing that you will never see your dead parent again. You might be angry at your parent for dying and leaving you and your family. You'll feel a sense of loss. That may make you sad whenever you think of him or her. And you may even feel guilty about your parent's death. You may think that the death was somehow your fault.

After losing a parent, children sometimes blame themselves for the death. You may think that if you

had not upset your parent, he or she would not
have died. But you did not cause your parent's
death. Your behavior had nothing to do with it.
People can't control when someone dies. You can't
always control your feelings, either. You'll need to
"mourn" (feel sad about the death of) your parent
in your own way and in your own time.

Everyone has a different way of mourning for a
loved one. Some people cry a lot. Others cry only
when they are alone. And some people don't cry at
all. If you feel like crying, don't hold back. If your
grief is quiet, that's okay, too. There is no right or
wrong way to mourn—there is only your own way.

Carrying On

When one parent dies, the surviving parent has
lost a lover and lifetime partner, as well as the
parent of their children. Like you, your parent will
mourn this terrible loss in his or her own way.
Mourning helps those who loved someone who has
died. It gives them a chance to express and release
all their emotions about that person. Expressing
these feelings of loss is a survivor's first step in
carrying on his or her life.

The death of a parent is a tragedy for the whole
family. But going through a difficult time often
brings people closer together. You, your brothers
and sisters, and your living parent may find new
strength in this closeness. This strength can help
you all get on with your own lives.

Chapter 5

"Things Will Never Be the Same"

Change is often hard to deal with. Over time, you become comfortable with the people you live with and see every day. You get used to the places where you live, work, play, and study. Making changes in your family or group of friends is not something you probably want to do.

Few things change your life in as many ways as a divorce or the death of a parent. Getting used to these changes is very important for everyone in your single-parent family. No one in the family can be happy until they have adjusted to the loss of the absent or deceased parent.

Missing Your Absent Parent

One of the hardest things to get used to after divorce or the death of a parent is the new order of your life. All of a sudden you can't see both of your parents every day.

If your parents have divorced, you may still be able to see your absent parent regularly. He or she may visit you often, or you may spend weekends with him or her. If possible, try to talk to your absent parent about how the divorce has made you feel. Explain that you still love and miss him or her. Explain that you are sad about the divorce. Also, tell your parent that although you may not understand the reasons, you are trying to accept the divorce. You know that both your parents needed to divorce in order to be happy.

The Question Is "Why?"

The death of a parent may be more difficult to accept than the loss of a parent through divorce. After a divorce, a child knows that the absent parent is still alive and there for him or her. But when a parent dies, the child knows he or she will never see the parent again. People often ask one question when a loved one dies: "Why?" That is a question no one can answer.

We cannot control death. And we can't explain why it occurs when it does. What we can do is try to accept that someone we love is gone forever. You can remember all the reasons why you loved— and still love—that person. After your time of grief has passed, you can carry on with life. You know that your loved one would have wanted you to do that.

Most children who lose a parent feel as if life is terribly unfair, and they wonder why it had to happen in their family.

Life Goes On

Whether you have lost a parent to death or to divorce, life in your new single-parent family must go on. It may take some time for you to adjust to life without your missing parent. You may be living in a new house or community. There will probably be less money to spend than before. Your single parent may be working longer hours, or just starting to work. This may add new responsibilities to your life.

Tara's mother had been single for years when she married again. Tara describes the effects on her family's lifestyle when her mom's second marriage failed.

"I was happy when Mom got married again. I was tired of living the way we were. When she married Ted, we moved into a nice house. We had money, and we didn't have to worry about whether the refrigerator was full. But since Mom and Ted got divorced, I'm totally sad. It's back to the old fight. Mom's been working really hard, and we're still not making it."

Your parent's longer work hours away from home may mean you will have to help more around the house. You may have to help with household chores or help take care of younger brothers or sisters. If you are home from school while your

Single-parent families often need children to take on more responsibilities, such as cleaning, cooking, and shopping.

single parent is working, you may be spending more time at home alone than before. You may become one of America's millions of "latchkey children." Those are children who come home and let themselves into an empty house. The house is empty because the parent(s) are still at work.

"Latchkey children" have to let themselves into their homes
after school because their parents are away or still at work.

Chapter 6

Life as a Latchkey Child

The phrase *latchkey children* comes from the key that many children wear on a cord around their neck. They need the key to let themselves into their home when their parents are away. Studies have shown that almost 20% of American families have children who spend part of the day at home alone. In the United States, over 5 million kids are latchkey children.

Many working parents—some single, some married—are still at their jobs when their kids come home from school. They have to work on school holidays and during vacations. It is hard for these parents to take time off from work. Few places have adults to supervise these children after school lets out. So most latchkey children must stay at home by themselves.

Alan's mom, a single parent, came home from work every day several hours after Alan and his sister got home from school. He remembers what being a latchkey kid was like for him and his sister.

"When we were younger, we had baby-sitters. But when we got a little older Mom gave us a key and we let ourselves in. We knew Mom had to work to pay the bills. My sister and I always kept busy. There were a lot of kids in the neighborhood, so we always played outside. It was really kind of fun. We never had Mom nagging us."

If you are a latchkey child, there are several things you should think about. Some of these things are discussed on the following pages. Talk to your parent about them. Together, you can decide what to do to make your time at home alone safer and happier.

Being Safe and Secure

Your parent wants to be sure that you are safe when you're home alone. This means being aware of things that can hurt you. If you know about dangerous things, you can prevent them from harming you. The world outside your home can sometimes be a dangerous place. Staying at home alone can be frightening too, especially for younger children. To *be* safe and *feel* safe and secure, you should follow a set of rules when you are at home alone. If you don't have rules, ask your parent to help you make a list. The list should include the following:

• *Take care of your key.* Don't wear it where everyone can see it. Try not to lose it. And know ahead of time where a spare key is hidden, in case you need it.

• *Lock the door after you get home.* If you are at home alone all day (on a school vacation day, for instance), keep the door locked while you're at home or when you go out.

• *Call your parent as soon as you get home from school.* He or she will want to know that you've arrived home safely. Make sure you have your parent's work phone number. Post it near the phone, so you can always find it. If you are at home alone all day, check in with your parent several times. And always call in case of an emergency.

• *Don't let anyone into the house.* If someone comes to the door, don't open it. Ask who it is. Open the door only for a family member. If you don't know who it is, never open the door.

• *Don't tell people that you are alone in the house.* If someone calls on the phone for your parent, say that he or she is busy and will call back later.

• *Don't cook anything or use electrical appliances* (unless you are older and have been taught how by your parent). Make snacks that don't need cooking.

• *Be prepared for emergencies.* Know where your family's first-aid kit is. Be sure that emergency numbers (fire, police, ambulance, your parent's place of work) are posted near the phone. Know how to call them in case you or someone else in your family is sick or has an accident.

• *Obey the "going out" rule.* Your parent will decide whether you can go outside when you are home alone. This will depend on where you live and how long you will be alone each day. If your parent decides it is safer for you to stay inside, you should do so.

All of these rules should be followed to ensure your safety as a latchkey kid. It is your parent's job to tell you what the rules are. You can help by talking about this chapter with your parent. But it is your job to follow these rules when you and your brothers and sisters are at home alone.

I'm Okay Alone

There are many things you can do to make the time your parent is at work more comfortable. Find out what after-school activities there are in your school or community center. These activities might include sports, scouting, or other groups or clubs. Ask your parent for permission to join in some of these activities. After-school groups can help fill the hours when you might otherwise be at home alone.

It is important for latchkey kids to keep in touch with their parents while the parents are not at home.

If you have to be at home alone, try to find things to do until your parent comes home. This might be a good time to get your homework done. But sometimes doing homework without a parent around to help you can be frustrating.

When you're at home alone, you might try to do as much of your homework as you can without help. When your parent comes home, ask him or her to check your work and to help you with the harder parts. Doing this every day gives you a chance to talk to your mom or dad about what you are learning in school. It also lets your parent know the areas in which you need help.

Some latchkey children watch a lot of television. TV provides more than entertainment and information. It can also be a kind of companion, helping you to feel less alone. But if you can't go out, there are things you can do other than watching TV. You may have chores to do around the house every afternoon. You can also read a book. You can listen to the stereo or the radio. Or you can talk with friends on the phone.

It is important for you to tell your parent how you feel about being at home alone. If being home alone makes you unhappy, say so. If you are a latchkey child now, your parent's job and responsibilities probably give him or her little choice in the matter. But talk about it. At least you and your parent will understand each other's feelings about the situation.

Chapter 7

Understanding Your Parent

It's easy to take your parent for granted. It may not seem that they have such a hard time taking care of you. But the truth is, even in two-parent homes, taking care of a family is a very difficult and complex responsibility. In a single-parent home there are even more things to deal with, and only one person to deal with them. A single parent has many responsibilities and a lot to worry about.

A Parent's Needs

Your parent probably spends most of his or her time and attention taking care of the needs of your family. There is little time left for his or her own needs. But that doesn't mean the needs aren't there. Your parent may need to spend some time away from the house, or may have other interests such as hobbies, sports, education, or dating.

Your parent needs relationships with other adults. He or she needs friends as well as dates. And your parent also needs time alone. These are just the things that are difficult for single parents to find the time for. Your help and understanding might make it easier for your parent to find ways to fill those needs.

Friends

Friends are important to all of us. Your friends may be as important to you as your family. Parents need friendships too. They need to enjoy the company of other adults. Sometimes single parents might find meeting people their own age difficult. They often spend all their free time with their children. It might be very tough for them to meet people their own age.

Rita, a single mother, recalls her need for adult companionship after several years of caring for her two young children alone. She tells how she decided to meet people.

My husband left me with two children under the age of two. I went to work full time once they were both in school. But having very little contact with adults was starting to get to me even before that. I love my children, but I couldn't take being surrounded by nothing but kids and kids' things any more. So I enrolled in a college course at night. I kept it up, one course at a time, even after I started working. Twelve years later, I got my degree.

Sometimes it's hard to accept that your parents need new relationships with other people in order to be happy.

If you can help your parent with the chores, instead of leaving everything for him or her to do, your parent will appreciate it. He or she will have more time to spend on his or her needs, and will be a happier person.

Coming Back to Life

Parents who have recently become single have a different problem. Often, the death or divorce that made them single and the difficult time following it may make them feel depressed. They may become withdrawn, or have very little self-confidence. Your parent may not want to be with other adults, or even with anyone. And people who were friends of both your parents may feel awkward around them now. This makes it hard for your newly single parent to get back into a social life again.

Your single parent needs your help and understanding now more than ever before. If you are uncontrollable and angry all the time, your parent will never have the chance to recover from the trauma your family has suffered. Try to cheer your parent up, try to help him or her out. Don't leave your parent in the cold.

Mixed Emotions

After a death or divorce it may be hard for you to accept that your parents are dating other people. You might feel that they are cheating on each other. It wasn't so long ago that they were still married.

However, you have to accept that your parents are no longer married. Everyone needs companionship in their lives, and your parents are no exception. Do not tell yourself that they are going to get back together, because the odds are they won't.

Time Alone

Parents need to relax and enjoy some of the things they like to do in peace and quiet. This can be hard to remember. It's easy to forget that your parent is a person too, not just put on this earth to take care of you.

You can help your parent find time to be alone. Offer to help by doing a chore your parent would usually do. Tell your younger brothers and sisters to come to you with a problem, instead of to your parent. Your parent will appreciate your love and understanding, and will find a better balance between being a parent and a person.

You may feel that your family is the only one that argues, but every family has conflicts.

Chapter 8

We're in This Together

Like any family, your single-parent family is bound to have its ups and downs. There will be times when you are angry with your parent, and he or she with you. All families argue. Conflicts will arise whether your parent has always been single or has just recently been divorced or widowed. Sometimes you may get frustrated and angry with other members of your family. Everybody has bad days. But it might seem to you that you have more than your share.

Adolescence

If you often feel that your life is going from bad to worse, you are not alone. You may be going through a difficult time that all teenagers go through—adolescence. Adolescence is the time in your life when you grow from childhood into adulthood. This growth is both physical and emotional. The process usually takes place during your teenage years. It is slow and often emotionally painful.

Adolescents are often filled with doubts about themselves. They are usually worried about many things: their looks, their body changes, their awkwardness, their experiences with the opposite sex, their desire for independence, their dealings with adults and others in authority. In other words, adolescence can be a pretty confusing and miserable time for everyone.

Communicate!

If you and your single parent seem to be "at each other's throats," stop and think for a minute. Think about how much you and your single parent depend on each other. Think about how much you really love each other—no matter how often you may fight. Then think about how you and your parent (and your brothers and sisters) can work together as a team. The first step toward this teamwork is communication.

Sherri, who lives with her single mother, has had many problems in the past. She talks about the pros and cons of communication in their now close relationship.

"I think I spend too much time with my mother. She's always asking me if I'm okay, and what's going on with my life, and if I'm happy. She gives me too much attention. Partly because I used to have problems in school. We're like sisters in a way. She tells me everything, and I do the same. Sometimes it bothers me, because some of the things she tells me I feel that a daughter shouldn't know."

Sometimes communication between parent and child can get too close. This can happen if a parent is using the child as a substitute for an adult friend. Knowing personal details about your parent can make you uncomfortable. If you feel that communication is too close between you and your mom or dad, you need to say so.

Trust Me!

Trust is an important part of a good relationship between parents and their children. For a single parent who has been through a painful divorce, trusting another person—even his or her own child—is not easy. But in order to trust someone, you must first understand him or her. Sharing your feelings with someone is a good way to communicate and build trust. Think about the things that are important to you. And think about the feelings you have toward your family, your friends, and your school. Have you told your parent about those feelings lately? Have you asked about his/her feelings too?

Making a Tough Job Easier

At the beginning of this book we talked about your "special relationship" with your single parent. You may not have thought about your relationship with your parent in that way before. After reading this book, you can understand what your parent is going through while caring for a family alone. This understanding is important. It can lead to more communication, cooperation, and trust between you and your single parent. Maybe your help and understanding will make the tough job of a single parent just a bit easier for your mom or dad. And your special relationship will become even more special as the years go by.

Glossary—*Explaining New Words*

abusive Harmful or hurtful to another person.

adolescence The time between the ages of 11 and 21 when one is becoming an adult.

biological Natural; having to do with the body.

communication Process of making words, thoughts, and meanings clear to another person.

conflict A problem or dispute between people.

cooperation Act of working together toward a common goal.

crisis Emergency situation.

custody Responsibility for the care and control of children, usually following a divorce.

depression Sadness; feeling "down" all the time.

divorce The legal ending of a marriage.

emotional Having to do with feelings, especially with deep feelings.

frustration Discouragement; a sense of failure.

grief Deep sadness and sense of loss, as after a death.

guilt Feeling of self-blame for something.

joint custody Legal arrangement in which both parents share responsibility for the children following a divorce.

latchkey child A child who regularly spends unsupervised time at home alone while parent is away or working.

maturity Growth, or the state of being adult.

mourning Process of feeling sad about death; grieving.

sex Lovemaking, or sexual relations.

sibling Brother or sister; children of the same parent(s).

single-parent family A family with only one parent, or a parent without a partner.

stress Pressure and anxiety.

unique Special; one of a kind.

visitation rights Legal permission to visit children, granted to noncustodial parent following divorce.

widow A woman whose husband has died.

widower A man whose wife has died.

Where to Get Help

When you are feeling down or depressed, try to talk to your parent about what is bothering you. If your problem has something to do with your parent, you may feel uncomfortable talking about it with him or her. In that case, talk to an adult you trust, such as a teacher, clergyman, counselor, or other adult relative. Ask your school guidance office for help.

There may be a time when you feel so depressed you think about running away from home, or even about dying. If you, your parent, or one of your siblings feels this way, there are places you can call for help. Look in the Emergency Numbers section or the Yellow Pages of your phone book for the words CRISIS CENTER or MENTAL HEALTH CENTER.

If you or someone in your family is thinking about suicide, call 1-800-555-1212. Ask the operator for the number of a SUICIDE HOTLINE. The operator will give you another number beginning with 1-800. Call it right away, and someone will be there to help you.

There are also groups or organizations that help parents and families with problems. Some of these groups can help single parents share experiences and information to solve their special problems. One such group for single parents is Parents Without Partners. Your parent can get more information about a Parents Without Partners group in your area from your local community services office, or by contacting:

Parents Without Partners
7910 Woodmont Avenue
Suite 100
Washington, DC   20014
(202) 654-8850

For Further Reading

De Frain, John, with Judy Fricke and Julie Elmen. *On Our Own*. Lexington, MA: Lexington Books, 1987. This book is a "single parents' survival guide." It gives single parents and their families helpful information about many common problems.

Glassman, Bruce. *Everything You Need to Know about Stepfamilies*, rev. ed. New York: The Rosen Publishing Group, Inc., 1994. A discussion about different kinds of family groupings. The feelings and expectations when making difficult changes are explored.

Johnson, Linda Carlson. *Everything You Need to Know about Your Parents' Divorce*, rev. ed. New York: The Rosen Publishing Group, Inc., 1995. This book is a guide to help young people understand divorce as the beginning of a different kind of family life.

Long, Lynette and Thomas. *The Handbook for Latchkey Children and Their Parents*. New York: Arbor House, 1983. This book, by an educator and a counselor, gives practical information for working parents and their latchkey children who must spend time at home alone.

Okimoto, Jean Davies. *My Mother Is Not Married to My Father.* New York: G.P. Putnam's Sons, 1981. (Fiction) This story is told by Cynthia, a young girl whose father is divorced and is dating a woman Cynthia does not like.

Powledge, Fred. *You'll Survive!* New York: Charles Scribner's Sons, 1986. This book is a young people's guide to getting through the many problems of adolescence.

Spies, Karen. *Everything You Need to Know About Grieving*, rev. ed. New York: The Rosen Publishing Group, Inc., 1993. This book explains how and why people grieve. It offers ideas for dealing with painful feelings.

Index

63

About the Author
Richard E. Mancini has written and edited a variety of materials for young people, ranging from film study guides to an upcoming book on Native American history and culture. He is currently editing educational materials for Lifetime Learning Systems, Inc. Mr. Mancini lives in Connecticut and is the father of a "blended family" of four children.

Acknowledgments and Photo Credits
Cover photo by Chuck Peterson.
All other photographs by Mary Lauzon.

Design/Production: Blackbirch Graphics, Inc.